Prego®

EASY ITALIAN RECIPES

HOMEMADE TASTE!
IT'S IN THERE.®

Prego's Easy Italian Recipes was produced by the Publishing Division of Campbell Soup Company, Campbell Place, Camden, NJ 08103-1799.

Corporate Editor:	Pat Teberg
Assistant Editors:	Alice Joy Carter, Ginny Gance, Margaret Romano
Marketing Manager:	Srini Sripada
Public Relations Manager:	Ginny Marcin
Campbell Kitchens:	Linda Armor, Joanne Fullan, Kathleen Johnston
Photography:	Peter Walters Photography/Chicago
Photographers:	Peter Walters, Peter Ross
Photo Stylist/Production:	Betty Karslake
Food Stylists:	Amy Andrews, Lois Hlavac, Moisette McNerney

Designed and published by Meredith Custom Publishing Services, 1912 Grand Avenue, Des Moines, IA 50309-3379. Printed in Hong Kong.
First Trade Paperback Edition 1996.

Pictured on the front cover: Chicken Parmesan *(page 70).*

Preparation and Cooking Times: Every recipe was developed and tested in the Campbell Kitchens by professional home economists. Use "Chill Time," "Cook Time," "Prep Time," "Stand Time" and/or "Thaw Time" given with each recipe as guides. The preparation times are based on the approximate amount of time required to assemble the recipes *before* baking or cooking. These times include preparation steps, such as chopping; mixing; cooking rice, pasta, vegetables; etc. The fact that some preparation steps can be done simultaneously or during cooking is taken into account. The cook times are based on the minimum amount of time required to cook, bake or broil the food in the recipes.

For sending us glassware, flatware, dinnerware, oven-to-tableware, cookware and serving accessories used in recipe photographs, a special thanks to: *Corning Consumer Products Company,* Corning, NY on page 49; *Dansk International Designs Ltd.,* Mount Kisco, NY on pages 19, 51 and 89; *The Denby Pottery Company,* New York, NY on pages 47 and 55; *Mikasa,* Secaucus, NJ on pages 39 and 83; *Nikko Ceramics, Inc.,* Wayne, NJ on pages 11, 45, 79, 86 and 87; *Oneida Silversmiths,* Oneida, NY on page 55; *The Pfaltzgraff Co.,* York, PA on pages 20-21, 33, 74 and 75; *Reed & Barton Silversmiths,* Taunton, MA on pages 29, 45, 61, 63 and 81; *Regal Ware, Inc.,* Kewaskum, WI on page 41; *Royal Worcester and Spode,* Moorestown, NJ on pages 63, 85 and 91; *Swid•Powell,* New York, NY on pages 29, 31, 43, 51, 53 and 67; *Taitù,* Dallas, TX on pages 19, 56-57, 61, 65 and 93; *Villeroy & Boch,* Princeton, NJ on pages 69, 73 and 81.

Prego

EASY ITALIAN RECIPES

COOK'S GUIDE — AN ITALIAN GLOSSARY

AL DENTE — Term used to describe perfectly cooked pasta, which literally means "to the tooth." Pasta should have a slight "bite" or chewiness to it, so start testing for doneness at the *minimum* cooking time given on the package.

ANCHOVIES — Small saltwater fish common to the Mediterranean Sea. Anchovy fillets can be flat or rolled, canned or bottled in oil or brine. Anchovies add a rich, intense fish flavor to many Italian recipes.

ANTIPASTO — This can be any assortment of hot or cold appetizers served "before the pasta" or before the meal.

BASIL — An Italian herb with fragrant leaves and a sweet, spicy taste used to add a zesty flavor to meats, poultry, soups, tomato sauce, sauces, stews and vegetables. Fresh basil leaves are more potent than the dried leaves.

BAY LEAVES — Green, aromatic, shiny leaves with a pungent, woodsy flavor. Adds flavor to meats, soups, stews and vegetables. Remove leaf before serving.

CACCIATORE — Literally meaning "hunter-style" or hearty, this term describes any meat dish usually prepared with mushrooms, tomatoes, herbs and wine.

CALZONE — Meaning "stuffed stocking," this is a circle of dough that is folded in half over a filling of cheese, meat or vegetables, then either baked or deep-fried.

CAPERS — The pickled flower buds of the caper bush often used in sauces and salads or as a garnish. Look for capers in jars near the olives in your supermarket.

CHIANTI WINE — The most popular Italian dry red wine, which is excellent for cooking in or serving with meat dishes.

FAGIOLI — The Italian word for beans, usually cannellini (white kidney beans), but can also refer to ceci (garbanzo beans) or fava (fava beans).

FOCACCIA — A large, flat round loaf of Italian bread resembling a pizza. Can be served drizzled with olive oil and sprinkled with herbs or topped with vegetables, cheese or tomato sauce.

GARLIC — A pungent, aromatic bulb used as a flavoring in many traditional Italian recipes. Cloves of garlic are used either whole or minced.

GENOA SALAMI — A fine-grind salami, originally from Genoa, Italy, generally made from pork and moderately spiced.

MARINARA SAUCE — A highly-seasoned Italian tomato sauce made with olive oil, onions, garlic and oregano.

MOZZARELLA CHEESE — In Southern Italy, fresh mozzarella is made from water buffalo's milk; in the United States it is made from cow's milk. Fresh mozzarella is very soft and mild, while the factory-produced cheese has a chewy texture.

OLIVE OIL — The cornerstone of Italian cooking. Olive oil is *graded* according to acidity levels. The deep-green extra-virgin olive oil, which is the most expensive, is only 1% acid; it is best used in small amounts for salads and added to recipes just before serving as the flavor deteriorates when heated. Pure or virgin olive oil is a lower grade more suitable for cooking. Store oil in a cool, dark place for up to six months or refrigerate up to one year.

OREGANO — An aromatic herb with small green leaves. It has a strong, pungent, slightly bitter flavor.

PARMESAN CHEESE — A hard, dry cheese from the Parma section of Italy. It is made from cow's milk and has strong, sharp flavor. Excellent for grating and best if aged for at least one year.

PARSLEY (ITALIAN) — A flat-leaved, flavorful parsley with a distinctive taste more suitable to cooking than the curly-leaved variety.

PEPPERONI — Highly seasoned with black and red pepper, this Italian hard salami is made of pork and beef. Typically used as a topping on pizza, it is often found in appetizers and sandwiches.

PROVOLONE CHEESE — A cheese with firm texture and a smoky flavor. When it ages, its flavor becomes more pungent. Provolone perks up baked dishes and hearty sandwiches.

RICOTTA CHEESE — Fresh, soft cheese similar to cottage cheese. It is actually a cheese by-product made from the whey that is drained off when other cheese is made.

ROMANO CHEESE — Made from sheep's milk, this is a firm, dry cheese with a strong flavor and is perfect for grating.

SAUSAGE — Sweet Italian sausage is made with coarsely ground pork and seasoned with salt, pepper and black peppercorns. Hot Italian sausage is seasoned with fennel seeds, red pepper flakes and spices. A ground turkey-based Italian sausage is also available.

SCALOPPINE — Small pieces of meat, usually veal cutlets, which are pounded thin into "scallops".

Sicilian Vegetable Pizza and *Meatball Sandwiches* (pages 8-9).

SNAPPY SNACKS, SANDWICHES & PIZZAS

Prego Spaghetti Sauces point the way to fabulous, unforgettable finger foods! Now you can turn *Meatball Sandwiches, Italian Sausage Sandwiches* and *Calzone* into pocket passions in minutes. And, Prego's visible herbs and spices and delicious homemade taste will turn *Sicilian Vegetable Pizza* into something more than a square meal! *Delizioso!*

Meatball Sandwiches

2   cups PREGO Spaghetti Sauce with Fresh Mushrooms
1   pound frozen fully cooked meatballs (about 16 meatballs,
       1 ounce *each*)
4   long hard rolls, split
1   cup shredded mozzarella cheese (4 ounces)
     Grated Parmesan cheese

• In 3-quart saucepan, combine spaghetti sauce and meatballs. Over medium-high heat, heat to boiling. Reduce heat to low. Cover; cook 20 minutes or until meatballs are heated through, stirring occasionally.

• Serve on rolls. Sprinkle with mozzarella and Parmesan cheeses. If desired, garnish with assorted *sweet pepper strips*.

Makes 4 servings
Prep Time: 5 minutes • Cook Time: 25 minutes

Let Prego help you create a tasty
and super-easy dipping sauce for
meatballs, chicken nuggets,
mozzarella sticks and fish sticks.
Heat 1 cup Prego traditional
spaghetti sauce and 1 tablespoon
grated Parmesan cheese. Your big
and little dippers will love the flavor
Prego brings out in their favorite
snacks.

SICILIAN VEGETABLE PIZZA

1 tablespoon olive *or* vegetable oil
2 cups sliced fresh mushrooms (about 6 ounces)
1 medium onion, sliced (about ½ cup)
1 package (10 ounces) frozen chopped broccoli, thawed and well drained
1 cup PREGO Three Cheese Spaghetti Sauce
1 loaf (1 pound) frozen white bread dough, thawed
2 cups shredded mozzarella cheese (8 ounces)

• Preheat oven to 400°F. Grease baking sheet.

• In 10-inch skillet over medium heat, in hot oil, cook mushrooms and onion until tender, stirring often. Add broccoli. Cook until liquid is evaporated, stirring often. Stir in spaghetti sauce. Remove from heat; set aside.

• On prepared baking sheet, press dough into a 12- by 10-inch rectangle, pinching up edges to form a rim. Bake 10 minutes or until lightly browned. Sprinkle *1 cup* cheese over crust to rim. Spoon spaghetti sauce mixture over cheese. Sprinkle with remaining *1 cup* cheese.

• Bake 10 minutes or until cheese is melted and crust is golden.

Makes 4 servings
Thaw Time: 8 hours • Prep Time: 20 minutes
Cook Time: 20 minutes

When it comes to enjoying pizza in the '90s, Americans have flipped for the modern stone-age variety! For crispy brick-oven pizza at home, bake pizza on a pizza stone and enjoy the authentic Old World taste and texture of a Friday night favorite!

Italian Sausage Sandwiches

  1   **pound Italian pork sausage, casing removed**
1½ **cups PREGO EXTRA CHUNKY Mushroom & Green Pepper**
        Spaghetti Sauce
  4   **long hard rolls, split**

• In 10-inch skillet over medium-high heat, cook sausage until browned, stirring to separate meat. Spoon off fat.

• Add spaghetti sauce. Reduce heat to low. Heat through, stirring occasionally. Serve on rolls. If desired, garnish with *green onion* and *carrot curls*.

Makes about 3 cups or 4 servings
Prep Time: 5 minutes • Cook Time: 10 minutes

Italian-Style Sloppy Joes: Prepare Italian Sausage Sandwiches as directed above, *except* substitute *1 pound ground beef* for the sausage. Add *1 medium onion*, chopped, while browning beef. Add *1 tablespoon Worcerstershire sauce* with spaghetti sauce. Serve on *6 hamburger buns*, split and toasted. Makes about 3 cups or 6 servings.

Mild and sweet or hot and sultry, Italian Sausage Sandwiches could be the perfect link between your hectic schedule and dinnertime! For a gobbling-good alternative, look for newly available Italian turkey sausage.

Cheese Pizza

1   package (10 ounces) refrigerated pizza crust
¾   cup PREGO Traditional Spaghetti Sauce
1½ cups shredded mozzarella cheese (6 ounces)

• Preheat oven to 425°F. Grease baking sheet.

• Unroll crust on prepared baking sheet. Press into 12- by 10-inch rectangle, pinching up edges to form a rim. Spread spaghetti sauce over crust to rim; top with cheese.

• Bake 12 minutes or until cheese is melted and crust is golden.

Makes 4 servings
Prep Time: 10 minutes   •   Cook Time: 12 minutes

English Muffin Pizzas: Substitute *4 English muffins*, split and toasted, for refrigerated pizza crust and increase spaghetti sauce to 1 cup.

Crusty Bread Pizza: Substitute *1 loaf (about 14 ounces) French or Italian bread*, split and toasted, for refrigerated pizza crust and increase spaghetti sauce to 1 cup.

Extra-Easy Pizza: Substitute *1 Italian bread shell* (about 16 ounces) for refrigerated pizza crust.

Try to top this! Pepperoni, sausage, ground beef, diced vegetables, mushrooms and olives are some of the most requested toppings for pizza, a food once considered "peasant fare."

Cheese Pizza *(top left)*
Extra-Easy Pizza *(top right)*
English Muffin Pizzas *(bottom)*

CALZONE

1 loaf (1 pound) frozen white bread dough, thawed
½ cup PREGO Spaghetti Sauce Flavored with Meat
½ cup thinly sliced pepperoni (2 ounces)
1½ cups shredded mozzarella cheese (6 ounces)

• Preheat oven to 400°F. Grease baking sheet.

• On lightly floured surface, roll dough into a 14-inch circle. Place on prepared baking sheet.

• Spread spaghetti sauce over *half* of dough within 1 inch of edge. Top with pepperoni and cheese. Fold dough over filling. Seal edge with fork. (Use fork in criss-cross fashion to make decorative edge, if desired.)

• Bake 20 minutes or until golden. Let stand 5 minutes. If desired, garnish with *fresh oregano.*

Makes 4 main-dish or 8 appetizer servings
Thaw Time: 8 hours • Prep Time: 10 minutes
Cook Time: 20 minutes • Stand Time: 5 minutes

Meaning "stuffed stockings," calzones are large circles of dough that are folded in half over a generous filling, sealed, then baked. All the flavors of a pepperoni pizza are "rounded out" in this palate-pleasing pocket. Let stand for 5 minutes before slicing.

CHICKEN MOZZARELLA SANDWICHES

1½ cups PREGO Three Cheese Spaghetti Sauce
  4 refrigerated fully cooked breaded chicken cutlets (each about 3 ounces)
  4 slices mozzarella cheese (each about 1 ounce)
  4 round hard rolls, split

• In 10-inch skillet over medium-high heat, heat spaghetti sauce to boiling. Arrange chicken in sauce. Reduce heat to low. Cover; cook 5 minutes or until chicken is heated through, stirring occasionally.

• Top chicken with cheese. Cover; heat until cheese is melted. Serve on rolls. If desired, serve with *seasoned French fries* and *Vlasic or Early California pitted Ripe Olives* and *Vlasic original Bread & Butter Pickles.*

Makes 4 servings
Prep Time: 5 minutes • Cook Time: 10 minutes

CHICKEN PIZZA MUFFINS

  4 English muffins, split and toasted
  1 cup PREGO Traditional Spaghetti Sauce
  2 cans (5 ounces *each*) SWANSON Chunk Chicken, drained
  1 cup shredded mozzarella cheese (4 ounces)
     Crushed red pepper, dried oregano leaves *or* garlic powder (optional)

• On baking sheet, arrange muffin halves. Spread each muffin half with *2 tablespoons* spaghetti sauce. Divide chicken and cheese evenly among muffin halves. Sprinkle with red pepper.

• Bake at 400°F. 10 minutes or until cheese is melted.

Makes 8 pizzas or 4 servings
Prep Time: 10 minutes • Cook Time: 10 minutes

Parmesan Bread Deluxe

1   **loaf (about 14 ounces) Italian bread**
½   **cup refrigerated MARIE'S Creamy Caesar Dressing and Dip**
⅓   **cup grated Parmesan cheese**
3   **tablespoons finely chopped green onion**

• Cut 24 (½-inch thick) slices from bread. (Reserve remaining bread for another use.)

• In small bowl, combine dressing, cheese and onion. Spread each bread slice with heaping teaspoon dressing mixture.

• On baking sheet, arrange bread slices. Broil 4 inches from heat 1 minute or until golden.

Makes 24 slices
Prep Time: 10 minutes • Cook Time: 5 minutes

Antipasto

½   **cup refrigerated MARIE'S Zesty Fat Free Italian Vinaigrette**
1   **jar (22 ounces) VLASIC Pepperoncini Salad Peppers, drained**
1   **can (6 ounces) VLASIC *or* EARLY CALIFORNIA pitted large Ripe Olives, drained**
8   **ounces provolone cheese, cut into cubes**
2   **cups fresh mushrooms cut in half (about 6 ounces)**
2   **cups cherry tomatoes cut in half**
4   **ounces pepperoni, sliced**
    Lettuce leaves

• Pour vinaigrette into large, shallow nonmetallic dish. Add peppers, olives, cheese, mushrooms, tomatoes and pepperoni. Toss to coat. Cover and refrigerate at least 30 minutes.

• Serve on lettuce.

Makes about 8 cups or 16 appetizer servings
Prep Time: 20 minutes • Chill Time: 30 minutes

Parmesan Bread Deluxe *(top)*
Antipasto *(bottom)*

PASTA PRESTO!

Suppertime satisfaction with an Italian accent and 100% homemade taste begins and ends with Prego's 28-ounce family-size jar! Pasta dishes like *Hearty Lasagna, Baked Ziti, Zesty Pasta 'n' Beef* and *Broccoli Stuffed Shells* have never been more exciting — or more inviting to your hungry household!

Vegetable Lasagna and
Hearty Ham 'n' Linguine
(pages 24-25).

PASTA GUIDE

There are so many interesting pasta shapes available. Be creative and try a new one in your favorite Italian recipes. However, certain pasta shapes and sauces complement each other. The choices are endless and the perfect combination is ultimately yours!

PASTA SHAPES	TYPES OF SAUCES
Chunky, short pasta (rotini, shells) or thicker spaghetti (like fettuccine)	Hearty meat or cream sauces
Long, thin pasta (angel hair, linguine) or small, short pasta (ditalini)	Light tomato or thin-coating sauces
Large tube-shape (rigatoni, ziti)	Hearty meat sauces
Small, delicate pastas (pastina, orzo)	Butter or cream sauces (good choice for soups)

BOW TIES

FETTUCCINE

PENNE

RIGATONI

CORKSCREW (Rotini)

LASAGNA

WAGON WHEELS

JUMBO SHELLS

COOKING PASTA

■ Use a large saucepot or Dutch oven and enough water (4 to 6 quarts of water) for one pound of dry pasta.

■ Bring the water to a rapid boil and gradually add pasta so water does not stop boiling. For long pasta goods like spaghetti, place ends in boiling water. As the pasta softens, it will gradually curl around the pot until it is all under water.

■ Boil, uncovered, stirring frequently to keep pieces separate. Follow package directions for cook times.

■ Start to test pasta for doneness at the *minimum* cook time given on the package. Perfectly-cooked pasta should be "al dente" or firm to the bite.

■ Drain in colander or strainer and serve immediately.

GENERAL PASTA COOKING TIPS

■ Fresh pasta cooks quickly, usually in just a few minutes.

■ Adding salt to the cooking water is a personal preference.

■ Adding oil to the cooking water is a personal preference. Oil does help to keep the pasta pieces separate during cooking; however, when pasta is coated with oil, it will not absorb sauce.

■ Rinsing pasta after cooking is not recommended because many important nutrients will be washed away. However, if the pasta is to be used in a cold salad, rinse briefly with cold water and drain again.

■ Cooked pasta may be refrigerated in an airtight container 3 to 5 days. Store cooked pasta and sauce separately.

■ The best pasta shapes for freezing are those that are used in baked recipes such as lasagna, ziti or manicotti. For make-ahead recipes, it is best to freeze the casserole before baking.

■ There are several ways to reheat cooked pasta: place in rapidly boiling water for 1 to 2 minutes; place in a microwave-safe dish, cover with vented plastic wrap and microwave on HIGH power 1 to 2 minutes; or place in colander and pour boiling water over it until heated through.

VEGETABLE LASAGNA

1   container (15 ounces) ricotta cheese
2   cups shredded mozzarella cheese (8 ounces)
2   eggs
4   medium carrots, shredded (about 2 cups)
1   package (10 ounces) frozen chopped broccoli, thawed and well drained
9   cooked lasagna noodles
1   jar (27.75 ounces) PREGO EXTRA CHUNKY Garden Combination
    Spaghetti Sauce (3 cups)
    Grated Parmesan cheese

• In large bowl, combine ricotta cheese, *1 cup* mozzarella cheese, eggs, carrots and broccoli; set aside.

• In greased 3-quart oblong baking dish, arrange *3* lasagna noodles. Top with *half* the vegetable mixture and *1 cup* spaghetti sauce. Repeat layers. Top with remaining *3* lasagna noodles and remaining *1 cup* spaghetti sauce. Sprinkle with remaining *1 cup* mozzarella cheese.

• Bake at 400°F. for 30 minutes or until hot and bubbling. Let stand 10 minutes. Serve with Parmesan cheese. If desired, garnish with *carrot flowers*, *fresh sage* and *fresh chives*.

Makes 8 main-dish servings
Prep Time: 25 minutes • Cook Time: 30 minutes
Stand Time: 10 minutes

"Whey" to go! Ricotta isn't really a cheese, but a by-product of other cheeses. Italian ricotta is made from the whey drained off during the making of mozzarella and provolone.

Hearty Ham 'n' Linguine

1   tablespoon olive *or* vegetable oil
1   cup finely chopped cooked ham
¼   teaspoon garlic powder *or* 2 cloves garlic, minced
1   jar (28 ounces) PREGO EXTRA CHUNKY Mushroom & Diced Tomato
      Spaghetti Sauce (3 cups)
½   cup coarsely chopped VLASIC *or* EARLY CALIFORNIA pitted
      Ripe Olives
½   cup grated Parmesan cheese
1   tablespoon red wine vinegar
6   cups hot cooked linguine (about 12 ounces dry)

• In 3-quart saucepan over medium heat, in hot oil, cook ham and garlic powder until ham is lightly browned, stirring often.

• Stir in spaghetti sauce, olives, *¼ cup* cheese and vinegar. Heat to boiling. Reduce heat to low. Cook 5 minutes, stirring occasionally. Serve over linguine. Serve with remaining ¼ *cup* cheese. If desired, garnish with additional *ripe olives* and *fresh parsley*.

Makes 4 main-dish servings
Prep Time: 10 minutes • Cook Time: 15 minutes

No, it's not a publication about the world's most pungent herb! The *garlic press* is a handy kitchen tool that takes the mess out of mincing garlic. Store garlic in a cool dry place inside a small wire basket or open jar. For best flavor, don't refrigerate.

Family Sausage Supper

1 pound Italian pork sausage, casing removed
1 jar (28 ounces) PREGO Spaghetti Sauce Flavored with Meat (3 cups)
½ cup sliced VLASIC *or* EARLY CALIFORNIA pitted Ripe Olives
⅛ teaspoon garlic powder *or* 1 clove garlic, minced
4 cups hot cooked bow tie macaroni (about 4 cups dry) *or* corkscrew macaroni (about 3 cups dry)
½ cup grated Parmesan cheese

• In 3-quart saucepan over medium-high heat, cook sausage until browned, stirring to separate meat. Spoon off fat.

• Add spaghetti sauce, olives and garlic powder. Heat to boiling. Reduce heat to low. Cook 5 minutes.

• Add macaroni and cheese; toss. Serve with additional cheese. If desired, serve with *green beans* and garnish with *radishes* and *fresh basil.*

Makes about 6 cups or 4 main-dish servings
Prep Time: 10 minutes • Cook Time: 20 minutes

Garden Pasta Toss

1 jar (27.75 ounces) PREGO EXTRA CHUNKY Garden Combination Spaghetti Sauce (3 cups)
1 bag (16 ounces) frozen vegetable combination (broccoli, cauliflower, carrots)
2 cups cooked corkscrew macaroni (about 1½ cups dry)
Grated Parmesan cheese

• In 3-quart saucepan, combine spaghetti sauce and vegetables. Over medium-high heat, heat to boiling. Reduce heat to low. Cover; cook 15 minutes or until vegetables are tender-crisp, stirring occasionally.

• Add macaroni. Heat through. Serve with cheese.

Makes about 6 cups or 6 side-dish servings
Prep Time: 5 minutes • Cook Time: 20 minutes

ZESTY MEAT SAUCE

1   pound ground beef
1   jar (28 ounces) PREGO EXTRA CHUNKY Zesty Garlic & Cheese
       Spaghetti Sauce (3 cups)
6   cups hot cooked spaghetti (about 12 ounces dry)

• In 10-inch skillet over medium-high heat, cook beef until browned, stirring to separate meat. Spoon off fat.

• Add spaghetti sauce. Heat through, stirring occasionally. Serve over spaghetti. If desired, garnish with *flowering fresh basil.*

Makes 4 main-dish servings
Prep Time: 10 minutes • Cook Time: 10 minutes

Looking for the perfect pasta partner for Zesty Meat Sauce? Rigatoni, corkscrew, shells and ziti macaroni or fusilli and spaghetti would be great go-togethers!

Zesty Pasta 'n' Beef

1   pound ground beef
1   medium onion, chopped (about ½ cup)
1   jar (28 ounces) PREGO EXTRA CHUNKY Zesty Oregano
      Spaghetti Sauce (3 cups)
3   cups cooked wagon wheel macaroni (about 2 cups dry) *or* elbow
      macaroni (about 1½ cups dry)

• In 10-inch skillet over medium-high heat, cook beef and onion until beef is browned and onion is tender, stirring to separate meat. Spoon off fat.

• Add spaghetti sauce and macaroni. Reduce heat to medium. Heat through, stirring occasionally. If desired, serve with *grated Parmesan cheese, carrot and zucchini sticks* and *garlic bread.*

Makes about 6 cups or 4 main-dish servings
Prep Time: 10 minutes • Cook Time: 15 minutes

Pasta Vegetable Skillet

1   tablespoon vegetable oil
2   medium zucchini, sliced (about 3 cups)
1   jar (28 ounces) PREGO EXTRA CHUNKY Tomato, Onion & Garlic
      Spaghetti Sauce (3 cups)
4   cups cooked elbow macaroni (about 2 cups dry) *or* corkscrew
      macaroni (about 3 cups dry)

• In 10-inch skillet over medium heat, in hot oil, cook zucchini until tender-crisp, stirring often.

• Add spaghetti sauce and macaroni. Heat through, stirring occasionally.

Makes about 6 cups or 6 side-dish servings
Prep Time: 15 minutes • Cook Time: 10 minutes

PASTA WITH THE WORKS

½ cup thinly sliced pepperoni (2 ounces)
1 medium green pepper, cut into strips
2 cups PREGO Spaghetti Sauce with Fresh Mushrooms
⅓ cup VLASIC *or* EARLY CALIFORNIA pitted Ripe Olives cut in half
    (optional)
4 cups hot cooked corkscrew macaroni (about 3 cups dry)
1 cup shredded mozzarella cheese (4 ounces)
    Grated Parmesan cheese

• In 10-inch skillet over medium heat, cook pepperoni and pepper until pepper is tender-crisp, stirring often.

• Stir in spaghetti sauce and olives. Over medium-high heat, heat to boiling. Reduce heat to low. Cover; cook 10 minutes, stirring occasionally. Remove from heat.

• Add macaroni and mozzarella cheese. Toss to coat. Serve with Parmesan cheese. If desired, garnish with *fresh basil.*

Makes about 6 cups or 4 main-dish servings
Prep Time: 15 minutes • Cook Time: 25 minutes

Penne is a smooth or ridged tubular pasta with angular ends that can be substituted for corkscrew macaroni in this recipe. Translated, penne means "quill pen." Would the empire have crumbled had the ancient Romans known that the *penne* really is mightier than the sword?

CHEESY VEGETABLE MACARONI

1 tablespoon olive *or* vegetable oil
2 medium zucchini, sliced (about 3 cups)
1 jar (28 ounces) PREGO Three Cheese Spaghetti Sauce (3 cups)
4 cups cooked corkscrew macaroni (about 3 cups dry)
1 cup shredded mozzarella cheese (4 ounces)

• In 10-inch skillet over medium heat, in hot oil, cook zucchini until tender-crisp, stirring often.

• Add spaghetti sauce and macaroni. Heat through, stirring occasionally.

• Stir in cheese.

Makes about 6 cups or 4 main-dish servings
Prep Time: 15 minutes • Cook Time: 10 minutes

When selecting fresh zucchini, look for tender, glossy skins free from bruises and blemishes. Choose zucchini that are slender in diameter and about 6 to 7 inches long.

TORTELLINI VEGETABLE TOSS

1　jar (27.75 ounces) PREGO EXTRA CHUNKY Garden Combination
　　　Spaghetti Sauce (3 cups)
1　bag (16 ounces) frozen vegetable combination (broccoli, cauliflower,
　　　carrots)
4½　cups cooked cheese-filled tortellini (about 1 pound frozen) *or* 3½ cups
　　　cooked small cheese-filled ravioli
　　　Grated Parmesan cheese

• In 3-quart saucepan, combine spaghetti sauce and vegetables. Over medium-high heat, heat to boiling. Reduce heat to low. Cover; cook 15 minutes or until vegetables are tender-crisp, stirring occasionally.

• Add tortellini. Heat through. Serve with cheese. If desired, garnish with *fresh basil* and *carrot curl.*

Makes about 8 cups or 4 main-dish servings
Prep Time: 5 minutes • Cook Time: 25 minutes

And you thought Chubby Checker

invented the Twist in Philadelphia!

Originated in the city of Bologna,

tortellini or "little twists" are small

rings of pasta stuffed with meat or

cheese. You'll find them in the freezer

or refrigerator section

of the supermarket.

FETTUCCINE AL FRESCO

 1   **tablespoon vegetable oil**
½   **cup diced cooked ham (optional)**
 1   **medium onion, chopped (about ½ cup)**
⅛   **teaspoon garlic powder** *or* **1 clove garlic, minced**
 1   **jar (28 ounces) PREGO Spaghetti Sauce with Fresh Mushrooms
     (3 cups)**
¼   **cup chopped fresh parsley** *or* **1 tablespoon dried parsley flakes**
 6   **cups hot cooked fettuccine** *or* **spaghetti (about 12 ounces dry)**
     Grated Parmesan cheese

• In 3-quart saucepan over medium heat, in hot oil, cook ham and onion with garlic until onion is tender, stirring often.

• Add spaghetti sauce and parsley. Heat through, stirring occasionally. Serve over fettuccine. Serve with cheese.

**Makes about 4 cups or 4 main-dish servings
Prep Time: 10 minutes • Cook Time: 10 minutes**

Ancient civilizations believed that
wearing wreaths of parsley around
the neck protected against the effects
of drunkenness! Today, parsley plays
a more conservative role as a
flavoring and garnish.

Tomato Mac 'n' Cheese

1 can (10¾ ounces) CAMPBELL'S condensed Cheddar Cheese Soup
1 cup PREGO Traditional Spaghetti Sauce
⅓ cup milk
4 cups cooked elbow macaroni (about 2 cups dry)
  Grated Parmesan cheese

• In 3-quart saucepan, combine soup, spaghetti sauce and milk; add macaroni.

• Over medium heat, heat through, stirring occasionally. Serve with cheese. If desired, garnish with *cherry tomatoes* and *fresh herbs.*

Makes about 5½ cups or 5 side-dish servings
Prep Time: 20 minutes • Cook Time: 5 minutes

Cheddar Zucchini Skillet

2 tablespoons olive *or* vegetable oil
5 medium zucchini, sliced (about 7½ cups)
1 medium onion, chopped (about ½ cup)
¼ teaspoon garlic powder *or* 2 cloves garlic, minced
1½ cups PREGO Spaghetti Sauce with Fresh Mushrooms
½ cup shredded Cheddar cheese (2 ounces)

• In 10-inch skillet over medium heat, in hot oil, cook zucchini, onion and garlic until tender-crisp, stirring often.

• Add spaghetti sauce. Heat through, stirring occasionally. Sprinkle with cheese. Cover; heat until cheese is melted. If desired, garnish with *fresh chives.*

Makes about 5½ cups or 7 side-dish servings
Prep Time: 10 minutes • Cook Time: 15 minutes

Tomato Mac 'n' Cheese *(top)*
Cheddar Zucchini Skillet *(bottom)*

VEGETABLE POTATO TOPPER

2   cups PREGO Traditional Spaghetti Sauce
1   small green pepper, chopped (about ½ cup)
⅓   cup grated Parmesan cheese
1   bag (16 ounces) frozen vegetable combination (broccoli, cauliflower, carrots)
4   hot baked potatoes, split
½   cup shredded mozzarella cheese (2 ounces)

• In 3-quart saucepan, combine spaghetti sauce, pepper and Parmesan cheese; stir in frozen vegetables. Over medium-high heat, heat to boiling. Reduce heat to low. Cover; cook 15 minutes or until vegetables are tender-crisp.

• Serve over potatoes. Top with mozzarella cheese. If desired, garnish with *yellow cherry tomatoes* and *celery leaves*.

Makes about 4 cups sauce or 4 side-dish servings
Prep Time: 10 minutes • Cook Time: 20 minutes

Hearty Vegetable Potato Topper: Add *½ cup chopped pepperoni* to spaghetti sauce before cooking.

QUICK SPAGHETTI AND MEATBALLS

1   jar (48 ounces) PREGO Spaghetti Sauce Flavored with Meat (5 cups)
1   pound frozen fully cooked meatballs (about 16 meatballs, 1 ounce *each*)
8   cups hot cooked spaghetti (about 16 ounces dry)
    Grated Parmesan cheese

• In 4-quart saucepan, combine spaghetti sauce and meatballs. Over medium-high heat, heat to boiling. Reduce heat to low. Cover; cook 20 minutes or until heated through. Serve over spaghetti. Serve with cheese.

Makes 6 main-dish servings
Prep Time: 5 minutes • Cook Time: 25 minutes

Vegetable Potato Topper *(top)*
Quick Spaghetti and Meatballs *(bottom)*

Broccoli Stuffed Shells

    1   container (15 ounces) ricotta cheese
    1   package (10 ounces) frozen chopped broccoli, thawed and well drained
    1   cup shredded mozzarella cheese (4 ounces)
    ⅓   cup grated Parmesan cheese
    ¼   teaspoon pepper
    18 cooked jumbo pasta shells (about 8 ounces dry)
    1   jar (27.75 ounces) PREGO EXTRA CHUNKY Garden Combination
        Spaghetti Sauce (3 cups)

• In medium bowl, combine ricotta cheese, broccoli, *½ cup* mozzarella cheese, Parmesan cheese and pepper. Spoon about *2 tablespoons* into each shell.

• In 3-quart oblong baking dish, spread *1 cup* spaghetti sauce. Arrange stuffed shells in single layer in spaghetti sauce. Pour remaining *2 cups* spaghetti sauce over shells. Sprinkle with remaining *½ cup* mozzarella cheese.

• Bake at 400°F. for 25 minutes or until hot and bubbling. If desired, garnish with *fresh sage.*

Makes 6 main-dish servings
Prep Time: 25 minutes • Cook Time: 25 minutes

Freshly ground pepper has a sharper and spicier flavor than the pre-ground kind. Try using a pepper mill or grinder to crush black peppercorns for the pepper needed in this recipe. For even more variety, experiment with green and white peppercorns and rate the distinct intensity each brings to the food.

BAKED ZITI

1   jar (28 ounces) PREGO Traditional Spaghetti Sauce (3 cups)
1½ cups shredded mozzarella cheese (6 ounces)
5   cups hot cooked ziti macaroni (about 3 cups dry)
¼   cup grated Parmesan cheese

• In large bowl, combine spaghetti sauce, *1 cup* mozzarella cheese and macaroni. Spoon into 2-quart oblong baking dish. Sprinkle with remaining *½ cup* mozzarella cheese and Parmesan cheese.

• Bake at 350°F. for 30 minutes or until hot and bubbling. If desired, garnish with *tomato slices* and *fresh basil.*

Makes about 6 cups or 4 main-dish servings
Prep Time: 25 minutes • Cook Time: 30 minutes

Make-Ahead Tip: To freeze, prepare ziti but *do not bake.* Cover tightly with foil and freeze. Bake *frozen ziti*, uncovered, at 350°F. for 1 hour or until hot and bubbling. *Or,* refrigerate 24 hours to thaw. Bake thawed ziti, uncovered, at 350°F. for 45 minutes or until hot and bubbling.

Baked Ziti Supreme: In 4-quart saucepan over medium-high heat, cook *1 pound ground beef* and *1 medium onion*, chopped (about ½ cup), until beef is browned and onion is tender, stirring to separate meat. Spoon off fat. Stir in spaghetti sauce, *1 cup* mozzarella cheese and macaroni. Spoon into 3-quart oblong baking dish. Sprinkle with cheeses and bake as directed. Makes 6 main-dish servings.

A great party or buffet dish, Baked Ziti can be doubled easily. Just spoon into a 3-quart oblong baking dish and bake 45 minutes. For easier cleanup, use a disposable foil baking pan.

DOUBLE MUSHROOM LASAGNA

  1   **can (10¾ ounces) CAMPBELL'S condensed Cream of Mushroom Soup**
  ¼   **cup milk**
  ¾   **pound ground beef**
1½ **cups PREGO Spaghetti Sauce with Fresh Mushrooms**
  6   **cooked lasagna noodles**
  1   **cup shredded Cheddar cheese (4 ounces)**

• In small bowl, combine soup and milk; set aside.

• In 3-quart saucepan over medium-high heat, cook beef until browned, stirring to separate meat. Spoon off fat. Stir in spaghetti sauce.

• In 8-inch square baking dish, spread *1 cup* meat mixture. Top with *2* lasagna noodles; trim to fit. Top with *½ cup* soup mixture. Repeat layers twice. Sprinkle with cheese.

• Bake at 400°F. for 30 minutes or until hot and bubbling. Let stand 10 minutes. If desired, garnish with *bay leaves* and *sweet pepper strips*.

Makes 4 main-dish servings
Prep Time: 25 minutes • Cook Time: 30 minutes
Stand Time: 10 minutes

Double the mushrooms, double the flavor! You might even want to make a double batch of this recipe! Don't be surprised when this doubly delicious crowd-pleaser brings the entire gang back for seconds!

EXTRA-EASY SPINACH LASAGNA

1   container (15 ounces) ricotta cheese
1   package (10 ounces) frozen chopped spinach, thawed and well drained
2   cups shredded mozzarella cheese (8 ounces)
1   jar (28 ounces) PREGO Spaghetti Sauce Flavored with Meat (3 cups)
6   *dry* lasagna noodles
¼   cup water

• In medium bowl, combine ricotta cheese, spinach and *1 cup* mozzarella cheese; set aside.

• In 2-quart oblong baking dish, spread *1 cup* spaghetti sauce. Top with *3* lasagna noodles and *half* the spinach mixture. Repeat layers. Top with remaining *1 cup* spaghetti sauce. Slowly pour water around *inside edges* of baking dish. Cover.

• Bake at 400°F. for 40 minutes. Uncover; sprinkle with remaining *1 cup* mozzarella cheese. Bake 10 minutes more or until hot and bubbling. Let stand 10 minutes. If desired, garnish with *fresh basil.*

Makes 8 main-dish servings
Prep Time: 20 minutes • Cook Time: 50 minutes
Stand Time: 10 minutes

This recipe lives up to its Extra-Easy name! Take a shortcut and don't cook the noodles. Simply layer them, uncooked, with the other ingredients and bake according to directions. Now that's easy!

Hearty Lasagna

  3 **cups ricotta cheese**
  3 **cups shredded mozzarella cheese (12 ounces)**
  2 **eggs**
  1 **pound ground beef**
  1 **jar (48 ounces) PREGO Traditional Spaghetti Sauce (5 cups)**
12 **cooked lasagna noodles**
½ **cup grated Parmesan cheese**

• In large bowl, combine ricotta cheese, mozzarella cheese and eggs; set aside.

• In 3-quart saucepan over medium-high heat, cook beef until browned, stirring to separate meat. Spoon off fat. Stir in spaghetti sauce.

• In each of two 2-quart oblong baking dishes, spread *1 cup* meat mixture. Top each with *2* lasagna noodles and about *1¼ cups* cheese mixture. Repeat layers. Top with remaining *2* lasagna noodles and remaining meat mixture. Sprinkle with Parmesan cheese.

• Bake at 400°F. for 30 minutes or until hot and bubbling. Let stand 10 minutes. If desired, garnish with *fresh herbs* and *carrot curls*.

Makes 12 main-dish servings
Prep Time: 30 minutes • Cook Time: 30 minutes
Stand Time: 10 minutes

Make-Ahead Tip: To freeze, prepare lasagna but *do not bake.* Cover tightly with foil and freeze. Bake *frozen lasagna*, uncovered, at 350°F. for 1 hour 15 minutes or until hot and bubbling. *Or;* refrigerate 24 hours to thaw. Bake *thawed lasagna*, uncovered, at 350°F. for 50 minutes or until hot and bubbling. Let stand 10 minutes.

Neapolitan Pasta Shells

2 tablespoons vegetable oil
2 medium zucchini, sliced (about 3 cups)
2 cups sliced fresh mushrooms (about 6 ounces)
1 medium onion, chopped (about ½ cup)
¼ teaspoon pepper
2 cups PREGO Three Cheese Spaghetti Sauce
4 cups hot cooked medium shell macaroni (about 3 cups dry)
1 cup shredded mozzarella cheese (4 ounces)

• In 4-quart saucepan over medium heat, in hot oil, cook zucchini, mushrooms, onion and pepper until tender and liquid is evaporated, stirring often.

• Stir in spaghetti sauce and macaroni. Spoon into 2-quart casserole. Sprinkle with cheese. Bake at 350°F. for 30 minutes or until hot and bubbling.

Makes about 6 cups or 4 main-dish servings
Prep Time: 20 minutes • Cook Time: 30 minutes

Try substituting different small pasta shapes for the macaroni in this recipe. *Rotini* and *radiatore* work well. And, kids will be delighted with *ruote*—wagon wheel-shaped pasta.

Simmered Chicken
with Olives and *Italiano*
Turkey and Pasta (pages 58-59).

POULTRY
WITH PIZZAZZ

Chicken and turkey — they make timeless meals! So does Prego because you spend *less time* in the kitchen preparing contemporary poultry recipes with delicious homemade flavor and flair! *Simmered Chicken with Olives, Italiano Turkey and Pasta* and *Chicken Parmesan* are all here and great for every occasion where family and friends enjoy good company and good food.

SIMMERED CHICKEN WITH OLIVES

- **4** **chicken breast halves *or* 8 chicken thighs (about 2 pounds)**
- **⅛** **teaspoon pepper**
- **1** **tablespoon olive *or* vegetable oil**
- **1** **jar (28 ounces) PREGO Traditional Spaghetti Sauce (3 cups)**
- **½** **cup sliced VLASIC *or* EARLY CALIFORNIA pitted Ripe Olives**
- **4** **cups hot cooked fettuccine *or* spaghetti (about 8 ounces dry)**
-     **Chopped fresh parsley (optional)**

• Sprinkle chicken with pepper. In 10-inch skillet over medium-high heat, in hot oil, cook chicken 10 minutes or until browned on both sides. Remove; set aside. Pour off fat.

• In same skillet, combine spaghetti sauce and olives. Heat to boiling. Return chicken to skillet. Reduce heat to low. Cover; cook 30 minutes or until chicken is no longer pink, stirring occasionally.

• Serve over spaghetti. Sprinkle with parsley. If desired, garnish with *baby squash* and *fresh chives*.

Makes 4 servings
Prep Time: 10 minutes • Cook Time: 45 minutes

Mama Mia! While the world's largest producers of olives are Italy and Spain, the "mother of the olive industry" was an American named Mrs. Freda Ehmann. In 1895, Mrs. Ehmann, of Marysville, California, pickled her bumper crop of olives and sold them in grocery stores.

Italiano Turkey and Pasta

  2 tablespoons olive *or* vegetable oil
  1 pound turkey breast cutlets *or* slices, cut into strips
  1 medium onion, thinly sliced (about ½ cup)
  ½ teaspoon dried rosemary leaves, crushed
  1 jar (28 ounces) PREGO EXTRA CHUNKY Mushroom & Diced Onion
       Spaghetti Sauce (3 cups)
  2 tablespoons grated Parmesan cheese
  ⅛ teaspoon crushed red pepper (optional)
  6 cups hot cooked spaghetti (about 12 ounces dry)

• In 10-inch skillet over medium-high heat, in *1 tablespoon* hot oil, cook *half* of the turkey until browned, stirring often. Remove; set aside. Repeat with remaining turkey. Pour off fat.

• Reduce heat to medium. In same skillet in remaining *1 tablespoon* hot oil, cook onion and rosemary until tender.

• Add spaghetti sauce, cheese and pepper. Over medium-high heat, heat to boiling. Return turkey to skillet. Reduce heat to low. Heat through, stirring occasionally. Serve over spaghetti. If desired, garnish with *yellow tomatoes* and *fresh rosemary*.

Makes 6 servings
Prep Time: 10 minutes • Cook Time: 25 minutes

The Tower of Pisa isn't the only thing with some lean to it! This recipe teams pasta and turkey for a naturally lean entrée that will make the whole family sit up straight to enjoy!

CHUNKY CHICKEN-VEGETABLE SKILLET

1   tablespoon vegetable oil
1   pound skinless, boneless chicken breasts *or* thighs, cut into cubes
1   jar (28 ounces) PREGO EXTRA CHUNKY Mushroom & Diced Onion
      Spaghetti Sauce (3 cups)
2   small zucchini, sliced (about 2 cups)
4   cups hot cooked fusilli *or* spaghetti (about 8 ounces dry)
      Grated Parmesan cheese

• In 10-inch skillet over medium-high heat, in hot oil, cook chicken until browned, stirring often. Remove. Pour off fat.

• In same pan, combine spaghetti sauce and zucchini. Heat to boiling. Return chicken to skillet. Reduce heat to low. Cover; cook 5 minutes or until chicken is no longer pink.

• Serve over fusilli. Sprinkle with cheese. If desired, garnish with *fresh herbs.*

Makes 5 cups or 5 servings
Prep Time: 10 minutes • Cook Time: 20 minutes

Grate expectations? You won't be disappointed when you accent your Italian recipes with aromatic Parmesan cheese. In Italy, premium Parmesan cheeses are aged from 2 to 4 years. U.S. versions are aged to about 14 months. Store grated Parmesan tightly sealed in the refrigerator.

Chicken Mediterranean

1 tablespoon olive *or* vegetable oil
1 pound skinless, boneless chicken breasts, cut into strips
1 jar (28 ounces) PREGO EXTRA CHUNKY Zesty Mushroom with
    Extra Spice Spaghetti Sauce (3 cups)
2 tablespoons red wine vinegar
½ cup sliced VLASIC *or* EARLY CALIFORNIA pitted Ripe Olives
4 cups hot cooked spaghetti (about 8 ounces dry)

• In 10-inch skillet over medium-high heat, in hot oil, cook *half* of the chicken until browned, stirring often. Remove; set aside. Repeat with remaining chicken. Pour off fat.

• In same skillet, combine spaghetti sauce, vinegar and olives. Heat to boiling. Return chicken to skillet. Reduce heat to low. Heat through, stirring occasionally. Serve over spaghetti. If desired, garnish with *yellow cherry tomatoes, gooseberries* and *fresh sage.*

Makes 4 servings
Prep Time: 10 minutes • Cook Time: 20 minutes

Zesty Basil Chicken

1 tablespoon vegetable oil
4 skinless, boneless chicken breast halves (about 1 pound)
1 jar (28 ounces) PREGO EXTRA CHUNKY Zesty Basil Spaghetti Sauce
    (3 cups)
4 cups hot cooked rice *or* corkscrew macaroni

• In skillet over medium-high heat, in hot oil, cook chicken 10 minutes or until browned on both sides. Remove. Pour off fat.

• Stir spaghetti sauce into same skillet. Heat to boiling. Return chicken to skillet. Reduce heat to low. Cover; cook 5 minutes or until chicken is no longer pink. Serve with rice.

Makes 4 servings
Prep Time: 5 minutes • Cook Time: 20 minutes

COUNTRY-STYLE CHICKEN

    2 slices bacon
    4 skinless, boneless chicken breast halves (about 1 pound)
    1 medium onion, sliced (about ½ cup)
    2 cups PREGO EXTRA CHUNKY Mushroom & Green Pepper
         Spaghetti Sauce
    4 cups hot cooked rice
       Chopped fresh parsley

• In skillet over medium heat, cook bacon until crisp. Transfer to paper towels to drain. Crumble bacon; set aside.

• In skillet over medium-high heat, in *1 tablespoon* hot drippings, cook chicken 10 minutes or until browned on both sides. Remove chicken. Reduce heat to medium. In skillet, cook onion until tender-crisp.

• Add spaghetti sauce and reserved bacon. Over medium-high heat, heat to boiling. Return chicken to skillet. Reduce heat to low. Cover; cook 5 minutes or until chicken is no longer pink. Sprinkle with parsley. Serve over rice. If desired, garnish with *celery leaves* and *cherry tomatoes*.

Makes 4 servings
Prep Time: 10 minutes • Cook Time: 30 minutes

SAUCY BAKED CHICKEN

    2 pounds chicken parts
    2 cups PREGO EXTRA CHUNKY Garden Combination Spaghetti Sauce

• In 2-quart oblong baking dish, arrange chicken. Bake at 375°F. for 30 minutes. Pour off fat. Pour spaghetti sauce over chicken. Bake 30 minutes or until chicken is no longer pink. Stir sauce before serving. Serve over *spaghetti*.

Makes 4 servings
Prep Time: 5 minutes • Cook Time: 1 hour

Country-Style Chicken *(top)*
Saucy Baked Chicken *(bottom)*

Clock-Watcher Cacciatore

1 tablespoon vegetable oil
1 pound skinless, boneless chicken breasts *or* thighs, cut into cubes
1 jar (27.75 ounces) PREGO EXTRA CHUNKY Mushroom & Green
   Pepper Spaghetti Sauce (3 cups)

• In 10-inch skillet over medium-high heat, in hot oil, cook *half* of the chicken until browned, stirring often. Remove; set aside. Repeat with remaining chicken. Pour off fat.

• In same skillet, heat spaghetti sauce to boiling. Return chicken to skillet. Reduce heat to low. Cover; cook 5 minutes or until chicken is no longer pink. Serve over *macaroni* with *salad.*

Makes 4 servings
Prep Time: 10 minutes • Cook Time: 20 minutes

Easy Chicken-Vegetable Italiano

1 tablespoon vegetable oil
1 pound skinless, boneless chicken breasts, cut into strips
1 jar (28 ounces) PREGO Spaghetti Sauce with Fresh Mushrooms
   (3 cups)
1 bag (16 ounces) frozen vegetable combination
¼ cup grated Parmesan cheese

• In 10-inch skillet over medium-high heat, in hot oil, cook *half* of the chicken until browned. Remove. Repeat with remaining chicken. Pour off fat.

• In skillet, heat spaghetti sauce, vegetables and cheese to boiling. Reduce heat to low. Cover; cook 15 minutes or until vegetables are tender-crisp. Return chicken to skillet. Heat through. Serve over *spaghetti.* If desired, garnish with *fresh strawberry leaves.*

Makes 6 servings
Prep Time: 10 minutes • Cook Time: 35 minutes

Clock-Watcher Cacciatore *(top)*
Easy Chicken-Vegetable Italiano *(bottom)*

SAVORY CHICKEN

1   tablespoon olive *or* vegetable oil
4   skinless, boneless chicken breast halves (about 1 pound)
½   cup diced cooked ham
1   medium onion, sliced (about ½ cup)
1   medium green pepper, cut into thin strips (about 1 cup)
¼   cup Chianti *or* other dry red wine (optional)
2   cups PREGO EXTRA CHUNKY Garden Combination Spaghetti Sauce
½   cup coarsely chopped VLASIC *or* EARLY CALIFORNIA Pimento-
      Stuffed Olives
4   cups hot cooked parslied rice

• In 10-inch skillet over medium-high heat, in hot oil, cook chicken 10 minutes or until browned on both sides. Remove; set aside. Reduce heat to medium.

• In same skillet in hot drippings, cook ham, onion and pepper until ham is browned and vegetables are tender-crisp, stirring often. Add wine; cook 2 minutes.

• Add spaghetti sauce and olives. Over medium-high heat, heat to boiling. Return chicken to skillet. Reduce heat to low. Cover; cook 5 minutes or until chicken is no longer pink, stirring occasionally. Serve over rice. If desired, *serve with breadsticks* and garnish with *fresh currants* and *celery leaves*.

Makes 4 servings
Prep Time: 15 minutes • Cook Time: 30 minutes

Named for the Chianti region in
Tuscany, Italy, *chianti* is a red wine
known for its bold earthy flavor.

CHICKEN WITH MUSHROOMS

1 tablespoon vegetable *or* olive oil
4 chicken breast halves (about 2 pounds)
1 jar (28 ounces) PREGO EXTRA CHUNKY Mushroom & Diced Tomato
    Spaghetti Sauce (3 cups)
2 jars (about 4½ ounces *each*) sliced mushrooms, drained
¼ cup Burgundy *or* other dry red wine (optional)

• In skillet over medium-high heat, in hot oil, cook chicken until browned. Remove. Pour off fat.

• In skillet, heat remaining ingredients to boiling. Return chicken to pan. Reduce heat to low. Cover; cook 30 minutes or until chicken is no longer pink. Serve over *noodles*. If desired, garnish with *fresh mushrooms* and *fresh basil*.

Makes 4 servings
Prep Time: 5 minutes • Cook Time: 45 minutes

CHICKEN PARMESAN

4 skinless, boneless chicken breast halves (about 1 pound)
1 egg *or* 2 egg whites, beaten
½ cup plain *or* seasoned dry bread crumbs
2 tablespoons olive *or* vegetable oil
2 cups PREGO Traditional Spaghetti Sauce
½ cup shredded mozzarella cheese (2 ounces)

• Dip chicken into egg. Coat chicken with bread crumbs.

• In skillet over medium heat, in hot oil, cook chicken 10 minutes or until browned. Remove. Pour off fat.

• In same pan over medium-high heat, heat spaghetti sauce to boiling. Return chicken to skillet. Reduce heat to low. Cover; cook 5 minutes or until chicken is done.

• Top chicken with mozzarella cheese. Cover; heat. Serve over *spaghetti*. Sprinkle with *grated Parmesan cheese* and *fresh parsley*.

Makes 4 servings
Prep Time: 10 minutes • Cook Time: 25 minutes

Chicken with White Beans

1   **tablespoon vegetable oil**
4   **chicken breast halves (about 2 pounds)**
2   **cups PREGO Spaghetti Sauce with Fresh Mushrooms**
2   **cans (about 16 ounces *each*) white kidney beans (cannellini), drained**
1   **large onion, chopped (about 1 cup)**
¼   **teaspoon garlic powder *or* 2 cloves garlic, minced**
¼   **teaspoon pepper**

• In 10-inch skillet over medium-high heat, in hot oil, cook chicken 10 minutes or until browned on both sides. Remove; set aside. Pour off fat.

• In same skillet, combine spaghetti sauce, beans, onion, garlic powder and pepper. Over medium-high heat, heat to boiling. Return chicken to skillet. Reduce heat to low. Cover; cook 30 minutes or until chicken is no longer pink, stirring occasionally. If desired, serve with wilted *fresh spinach* and garnish with *fresh chervil* and *red pearl onions*.

Makes 4 servings
Prep Time: 10 minutes • Cook Time: 45 minutes

Cannellini beans, or white kidney

beans, are a mainstay in regional

Italian cooking, particularly in soups,

salads and stews.

FAMILY-PLEASING BEEF AND PORK

Who says meat and potatoes aren't Italian? Mouthwatering *Italian Pot Roast, Easy Beef Stew, Ravioli and Sausage,* and *Pork Chops Parmesan* are just a few of the recipes seasoned to Prego perfection! And, they're perfect for entertaining, too! The taste of Italy? *It's in there!*

Italian Pot Roast and
Prego Pork and Peppers (pages 76-77).

ITALIAN POT ROAST

  2 **tablespoons vegetable oil**
3½- to 4-pound boneless beef bottom round *or* chuck pot roast
  1 **jar (28 ounces) PREGO Traditional Spaghetti Sauce (3 cups)**
  6 **medium potatoes, cut into quarters (about 3½ cups)**
  6 **medium carrots, cut into 2-inch pieces (about 2 cups)**

• In 6-quart Dutch oven over medium-high heat, in hot oil, cook roast until browned on all sides. Spoon off fat.

• Add spaghetti sauce. Heat to boiling. Reduce heat to low. Cover; cook 1 hour 45 minutes, stirring occasionally. Add potatoes and carrots. Cover; cook 1 hour or until roast and vegetables are fork-tender, stirring occasionally. If desired, garnish with *tomato* and *fresh parsley.*

Makes 8 servings
Prep Time: 5 minutes • Cook Time: 3 hours

Yankee Doodle gets a Neapolitan spin with this pot roast recipe that's sensational for company, special occasions and Sunday dinner.

PREGO PORK AND PEPPERS

2   tablespoons olive *or* vegetable oil
6   pork chops, ¾ inch thick (about 2 pounds)
2   medium green peppers, cut into strips (about 2 cups)
1   medium onion, cut into 8 wedges
1   jar (28 ounces) PREGO Spaghetti Sauce Flavored with Meat (3 cups)
6   cups hot cooked egg noodles

• In 10-inch skillet over medium-high heat, in *1 tablespoon* hot oil, cook *half* of the chops 10 minutes or until browned on both sides. Remove; set aside. Repeat with remaining chops.

• Reduce heat to medium. In same skillet, in remaining *1 tablespoon* hot oil, cook peppers and onion until tender-crisp, stirring often.

• Stir in spaghetti sauce. Over medium-high heat, heat to boiling. Return chops to skillet. Reduce heat to low. Cover; cook 10 minutes or until chops are no longer pink, stirring occasionally. Serve over noodles.

Makes 6 servings
Prep Time: 10 minutes • Cook Time: 35 minutes

Extra-virgin is the most expensive of the numerous imported and domestic varieties of olive oil. Because the flavor breaks down when heated, the most expensive doesn't mean the best where cooking is concerned. Pure olive oil, also called virgin, is the most suitable for frying, broiling and baking.

ITALIAN-STYLE MEAT LOAF

1   cup PREGO Traditional Spaghetti Sauce
2   pounds ground beef
1½ cups PEPPERIDGE FARM Herb Seasoned Stuffing
2   eggs, beaten
1   large onion, finely chopped (about 1 cup)
½ cup shredded mozzarella cheese (2 ounces)

• In large bowl, mix *thoroughly* ½ *cup* spaghetti sauce, beef, stuffing, eggs and onion. In 2-quart oblong baking dish, *firmly* shape meat mixture into 8- by 4-inch loaf.

• Bake at 350°F. for 1 hour 25 minutes or until meat loaf is no longer pink. Spoon remaining ½ *cup* spaghetti sauce over meat loaf; sprinkle with cheese. Bake 5 minutes more or until cheese is melted. If desired, garnish with *red onion wedges* and *fresh sage.*

Makes 8 servings
Prep Time: 15 minutes • Cook Time: 1½ hours

Prego traditional spaghetti sauce

and Pepperidge Farm herb seasoned

stuffing team up to lend an Italian

accent to the classic all-American

family favorite. Buon Appetito!

ITALIAN PEPPER STEAK

1   **pound boneless beef sirloin** *or* **top round steak, ¾-inch thick**
2   **tablespoons olive** *or* **vegetable oil**
1   **cup green, sweet red** *and/or* **sweet yellow pepper strips**
1   **medium onion, sliced (about ½ cup)**
¼   **teaspoon garlic powder** *or* **2 cloves garlic, minced**
2   **cups PREGO EXTRA CHUNKY Mushroom & Green Pepper**
    Spaghetti Sauce
4   **cups hot cooked fettuccine** *or* **spaghetti (about 8 ounces dry)**

• Slice beef across the grain into thin strips.

• In 10-inch skillet over medium-high heat, in *1 tablespoon* hot oil, cook *half* of the beef until browned, stirring often. Remove; set aside. Repeat with remaining beef.

• Reduce heat to medium. In same skillet, in remaining *1 tablespoon* hot oil, cook pepper, onion and garlic powder until tender, stirring often.

• Stir in spaghetti sauce. Over medium-high heat, heat to boiling. Return beef to skillet. Heat through, stirring occasionally. Serve over fettuccine. If desired, garnish with *fresh sage* and *fresh oregano*.

Makes 4 servings
Prep Time: 15 minutes • Cook Time: 25 minutes

When cooking pasta, allow at least four quarts of water per pound. Bring water to a rapid boil and cook pasta, uncovered, for 7 to 10 minutes or until *al dente* (tender but still firm).

EASY BEEF STEW

1   **tablespoon vegetable oil**
1   **pound boneless beef sirloin steak, cut into ¾-inch cubes**
2   **cups PREGO Spaghetti Sauce with Fresh Mushrooms**
1   **large onion, coarsely chopped (about 1 cup)**
1   **bag (16 ounces) frozen Italian-style vegetable combination**
4   **cups hot seasoned mashed potatoes *or* hot cooked egg noodles**
    (about 4 cups dry)

• In 4-quart saucepan over medium-high heat, in hot oil, cook beef until browned, stirring often. Remove; set aside. Pour off fat.

• In same saucepan, combine spaghetti sauce and onion. Heat to boiling. Return beef to saucepan. Reduce heat to low. Cover; cook 35 minutes, stirring occasionally. Add frozen vegetables. Cover; cook 15 minutes or until meat and vegetables are tender. Serve over mashed potatoes. If desired, garnish with *fresh sage* and chopped *fresh parsley*.

Makes 4 servings
Prep Time: 5 minutes • Cook Time: 1 hour

If you're dancing as fast as you can to get dinner on the table, don't stew about it—do the Mashed Potato! Instant mashed potato flakes are the perfect time-saving partner for this mouthwatering recipe!

Ravioli and Sausage

½ pound Italian sausage, casing removed
1   jar (27.75 ounces) PREGO EXTRA CHUNKY Mushroom & Green
      Pepper Spaghetti Sauce (3 cups)
2   packages (about 14 ounces *each*) frozen cheese-filled ravioli, cooked
      and drained
      Grated Parmesan cheese

• In 10-inch skillet over medium-high heat, cook sausage until browned, stirring to separate meat. Spoon off fat.

• Add spaghetti sauce. Reduce heat to low. Heat through, stirring occasionally. Serve over ravioli with cheese. If desired, serve with peas and garnish with *fresh thyme*.

Makes 4 servings
Prep Time: 10 minutes • Cook Time: 15 minutes

Pork Chops Parmesan

¼   cup dry bread crumbs
¼   cup grated Parmesan cheese
⅛   teaspoon pepper
6   boneless pork chops, ¾ inch thick (about 1½ pounds)
1½ cups PREGO Traditional Spaghetti Sauce
1   cup shredded mozzarella cheese (4 ounces)

• On waxed paper, combine bread crumbs, Parmesan cheese and pepper. Coat chops with bread crumb mixture.

• In 3-quart oblong baking dish, arrange chops. Bake at 400°F. for 20 minutes or until chops are no longer pink.

• Pour spaghetti sauce over chops. Sprinkle with mozzarella cheese. Bake 5 minutes more or until sauce is hot and bubbling. If desired, serve over *hot cooked spaghetti* and garnish with *fresh marjoram* and *sweet yellow pepper strips*.

Makes 6 servings
Prep Time: 10 minutes • Cook Time: 25 minutes

Ravioli and Sausage *(top)*
Pork Chops Parmesan *(bottom)*

SIMPLY SAVORY SEAFOOD

When seafood goes Italian at your house, the tide of requests for these fish dishes will never ebb! Prego puts you in the swim with many savory recipes that surface on your table in 30 easy minutes or less. *Seafood Stew Provençal, Tuna Mac Bake* and *Mussels Marinara* are destined to become your family's favorite *current* events!

Mussels Marinara and *Seafood Stew Provençal* (pages 88-89).

MUSSELS MARINARA

3 pounds mussels (about 4 dozen)
1 jar (28 ounces) PREGO EXTRA CHUNKY Tomato, Onion & Garlic
    Spaghetti Sauce (3 cups)
4 cups hot cooked linguine (about 8 ounces dry)

• Discard any mussels that remain open when tapped with fingers. Scrub mussels; trim "beards" with kitchen shears if necessary and discard.

• In 4-quart saucepan over medium-high heat, heat spaghetti sauce to boiling. Reduce heat to low; add mussels. Cover; cook 10 minutes or until mussel shells open, stirring occasionally. (Discard any mussels that remain closed.) Serve over linguine. If desired, garnish with *fresh chives* and *lemon slices.*

Makes 4 main-dish servings
Prep Time: 15 minutes • Cook Time: 10 minutes

Clams Marinara: Prepare Mussels Marinara as directed above, except substitute *2 cans (6½ ounces each) minced clams, undrained,* for mussels.

When buying fresh mussels or clams,

select those with tightly closed shells,

or shells that snap shut when tapped.

This means they're alive and fresh.

Avoid those with broken shells. Store

fresh mussels and clams in the

refrigerator for up to two days.

Seafood Stew Provençal

8   small clams with shells, well scrubbed
2   cups PREGO EXTRA CHUNKY Mushroom & Green Pepper
     Spaghetti Sauce
1   bottle (8 ounces) clam juice
¼   cup Burgundy *or* other dry red wine (optional)
1   pound fish *and/or* seafood*
     Chopped fresh parsley

• Discard any clams that remain open when tapped with fingers.

• In 3-quart saucepan, combine spaghetti sauce, clam juice and wine. Over medium-high heat, heat to boiling. Reduce heat to low. Cook 5 minutes, stirring occasionally.

• Add fish and clams. Cover; cook 5 minutes or until fish flakes easily when tested with a fork and clam shells open, stirring occasionally. (Discard any clams that remain closed.)

• Sprinkle with parsley. If desired, garnish with *fresh parsley*.

Makes about 5 cups or 4 main-dish servings
Prep Time: 10 minutes • Cook Time: 15 minutes

*For 1 pound fish *and/or* seafood, use any combination of the following: Firm white fish fillets, cut into 2-inch pieces; boneless fish steaks, cut into 1-inch cubes; medium shrimp, shelled and deveined; *or* scallops.

Italian-flavored seafood, or *frutti de mare* (fruits of the sea), and the distinctive seasonings of regional Italy combine in your kitchen for a deliciously easy meal in minutes.

TUNA MAC BAKE

1   can (10¾ ounces) CAMPBELL'S condensed Cream of Mushroom Soup
½   cup milk
1½ cups PREGO Traditional Spaghetti Sauce
1   cup shredded Monterey Jack cheese (4 ounces)
⅓   cup grated Parmesan cheese
4   cups hot cooked medium shell macaroni (about 3 cups dry)
1   can (about 6 ounces) tuna, drained and flaked
½   cup PEPPERIDGE FARM Seasoned Croutons, coarsely crushed

• In medium bowl, combine soup and milk. Stir in spaghetti sauce, Monterey Jack cheese and Parmesan cheese. Add macaroni and tuna; toss gently to coat. Spoon into 2-quart oblong baking dish.

• Bake at 350°F. for 25 minutes. Top with croutons. Bake 5 minutes more or until hot and bubbling. If desired, garnish with *celery leaves* and assorted *sweet pepper strips*.

Makes about 6½ cups or 5 main-dish servings
Prep Time: 20 minutes • Cook Time: 30 minutes

Traditional tuna noodle casserole
goes Italian in this super-easy recipe
that's *molto bene* for meatless menus
all year 'round.

SAVORY SHRIMP AND MUSHROOMS

1   tablespoon olive *or* vegetable oil
1   medium onion, chopped (about ½ cup)
1   small green pepper, chopped (about ½ cup)
¼   teaspoon garlic powder *or* 2 cloves garlic, minced
⅛   teaspoon ground red pepper (cayenne), optional
1   jar (28 ounces) PREGO Spaghetti Sauce with Fresh Mushrooms
    (3 cups)
1   pound medium shrimp, shelled and deveined
6   cups hot cooked thin spaghetti *or* fusilli (about 8 ounces dry)
    Grated Parmesan cheese

• In 10-inch skillet over medium heat, in hot oil, cook onion, green pepper, garlic powder and red pepper until tender, stirring often.

• Add spaghetti sauce. Over medium-high heat, heat to boiling. Reduce heat to low. Add shrimp. Cover; cook 5 minutes or until shrimp turn pink, stirring occasionally. Serve over spaghetti. Sprinkle with cheese. If desired, garnish with *fresh rosemary.*

Makes about 5 cups or 4 main-dish servings
Prep Time: 25 minutes • Cook Time: 15 minutes

Shrimp is America's most popular shellfish. Boiled, fried, baked, broiled and barbecued, U.S. consumption of the compact crustacean amounts to about 2½ pounds per person annually.

Recipe Index

RECIPE INDEX CONTINUED

Recipes-By-Product Index